Cherry Berry

John Hacker

ISBN 979-8-89243-921-3 (paperback)
ISBN 979-8-89243-922-0 (digital)

Christian Faith Publishing
832 Park Avenue
Meadville, PA 16335
www.christianfaithpublishing.com

Printed in the United States of America

To my sweet Savannah; may the Lord bless you in every way!

To all the young children who are learning to read
and the ones that enjoy reading, enjoy life, and
everything that God surrounds you with!

Chiddy

Oh how she loves ice cream and cakes. "So delicious!" she exclaimed.

Chiddy enjoyed every bite and would not allow one drop to fall to the ground. Upon finishing, Chiddy would lick her hands clean with her tongue. Wow! Any flavor will do—chocolate, rocky road, chunky-monkey, double fudge, vanilla swirl cone with rainbow sprinkles, Neapolitan, mint chocolate chip, cookies and cream, cherry-berry, grape-nut—you name them. If she had ice cream yesterday, it seemed insufficient to satisfy her yearning. She was never hungry nor too full to partake of another big cone. This was one time when she wished her bigger sister was there to grant her satisfaction.

"Chiddy! Chiddy! Are you doing your homework? Your teachers are complaining that you are not finishing your assignments on time."

Mom promised Chiddy that if she finished her homework on time, she would buy a big bowl of her favorite foods and give her another huge surprise later.

"Hmmm, nice, this sounds like a good plan. Ice cream today and a big surprise tomorrow?" It was summer, and she wondered what the big surprise would be. "More and more of my favorite food? Or maybe she is planning another trip? Does it mean seeing Dad? I haven't seen Dad in a very, very long while. Hmmm. Let's see. Let me go and get all the work done as quickly as possible."

Meanwhile, she was whispering, humming, and muttering to herself.

Chiddy loves her mother more and would do anything to get her favorite treat. Hmmm! Her typical behavior is to forget when she makes important promises as quickly as she makes them. However, this time, something different was happening. She got on task with her assignment but was having difficulty concentrating as her mind was on her mother's promises.

Guess what? She was never going to lose this one bowl of ice cream today. As she settled down to work, she thought she heard the familiar sounds of chimes and children's songs of bells ringing in the distance.

Chiddy began to rub her hands together as she anticipated her treat being nearer than she thought. *Come on, come on, come on! Ice-cream truck.* She couldn't wait for the ice-cream truck to arrive already.

Closing her books and pacing the floor, she anticipated the long-awaited response from her mother, which took forever. Supposing the truck to be nearer, her anxiety increased as she hoped to be paid for all the hard work. She kept running back and forth to Mother with every imagined sound of the truck. Mother knew that Chiddy had stopped working. Preoccupied, she listened intently for the actual sounds of the truck to come by on her street.

Already waiting for her mother's permission to close the book, Chiddy was more than awake and ready. She could not spare enough time for the truck to arrive. Unfortunately, she realized the truck had skipped her street and went to the other street; Chiddy was very upset. She was furious by now, getting out of her mind. "How could they do this to me?" And she would not allow anything to deprive her of getting her treat today.

She would have to find another way to get to the truck to fulfill her longing, to satisfy her taste buds with the icy juicy taste of sweet, creamy, milky substance in her already watery mouth.

She would celebrate every time after devouring this creamy substance by saying, "Give me a shout! Give out a big shout! To ice cream! Ice cream!" She remembered the old saying, "Craving hurts puppy!" This means that being greedy makes one uncomfortable. But it didn't matter; nothing would get in her way. Ice cream it is; ice cream it would be.

The Obstacle

Rubbing hands together just after hearing the words ice cream, she exclaimed, "Ice cream! Ice cream! Oh how I want you; I love you morning, noon, and night." Oh how she loves the taste.

In the meantime, Mommy sat in the chair to rest her head and fell asleep. Chiddy tried to wake her, but she was too tired to open an eye. Again, Chiddy went over and shook Mom and called her name. "Mom! Mom!" But she did not make a single budge. This only angered the little girl more, and she would not let the truck go away without her final move. She ran to the next stop down the road to meet it. But then another problem raised its ugly head.

"Oh! What is it now? Yes!"

Everything was going against her today. This one was more upsetting than all the other obstacles. This posed a big, big problem. What do you think Chiddy did not have to get her favorite food? She had some. But it would not reach the amount needed—enough to purchase the belly-filling, sweet, juicy, milky taste. "I don't want to say."

Do you know what I am referring to?

"Yes! Ice cream? Money?"

Do you think she was happy about it? Do you think she will need to stop remembering this sometime soon?

Strange Voices

"**Y**es!" Most interesting, a little voice-like creature always seems ready to interrupt her imagination with exciting answers to her terrible thirst problem. Everyone hears voices all the time. However, it is essential to listen to the right one.

A tiny imaginary creature that stops on children's shoulders and whispers something strange is nothing new. But maybe she won't be listening to the little voice today. Will she? But it kept ringing like a bell in her ears. And as she listened carefully, it became more apparent.

What?

What?

See mother's bag sitting over there?

What is it telling her to do?

Spash-spash-spash-sssseeee, weeeeees.

The creature whispered. "Look over there. There is your mother's bag. The good thing is she was sleeping, and she will not miss one measly old dollar if you only take one anyway."

So Chiddy would learn an important lesson that day. Once more, the little girl looked out her window, heard the chimes, and saw the ice-cream truck slowly going in the other direction. She planned to catch it when it came around the corner. It stopped at Gingers' gate but took longer to leave. "What's keeping it?" the voice whispered.

Meanwhile, she calculated how fast she must hurry before it reached the next block. She wanted so badly to have an ice-cream cone. She rubbed her belly and hands together, her appetite rising and her stomach growling like a small stream of rolling water.

Touchy Hands

Anticipation lent her the better hand. She was not ready to let it go, even though they had many different foods in their house to satisfy. Only ice cream, she thought, could fulfill.

Chiddy looked both ways and gave her mother the final check. She tiptoed over to the bag and reached inside her mom's purse. She dug around and nervously pulled out a crisp, clean dollar bill.

It is funny how before doing bad things, almost everyone looked on either side but never looked up. Looking up is more important than any other look.

What went wrong here? She took the money without her mom's consent. And she thought to herself, *Wow! I'm going to get a vanilla swirl cone with rainbow sprinkles ice cream on her own for the first time.*

But…did it give her a good feeling? Bad feelings started to rush down her stomach. She could not understand what was happening at that time. It was the first time she had done something like this. She was sure that Mother would not be pleased about it.

Oh, boy, it felt like a sad butterfly was flying around in her head. She could not help but feel bad for taking the money without permission.

Bitter Ice Cream

Have you ever tasted bitter ice cream before? However, as she walked to catch up with the truck, she presented the dollar bill, and the man, in return, gave her one cone. Chiddy hurriedly grabbed the cone from his hands and immediately jumped with delight and joy. She received the cone with a big smile on her face. She closed her eyes and gently wiped her tongue and lips as she tasted her favorite treat. Her eyes glowed with anticipation as she walked along the other street, skipping and licking the juice before it melted and dripped all over her clothes.

Mission accomplished, done, done—jumping, bouncing, and pouncing around the street to reach home before Mom woke up and discovered she was missing.

Chiddy's imagination got the better of her reality. The sound of her mother's voice rang heavily. "What have you done, dear? You will be grounded for a week, and you will not be getting ice cream for a long time." It resonated louder as she ran and tried to hurry home.

Remember, Chiddy never dropped one tip of ice cream before. And how is it that the front of her clothes was painted cherry-berry mixed with vanilla swirl cone and rainbow sprinkles? It just didn't feel or taste good in her mouth anymore. It was as if her favorite cherry-berry ice-cream mix, which she loved, suddenly tasted sour and bitter. There was no really lovely taste in her mouth anymore.

She intended to sneak into the house before Mom woke up, bathe, and change her clothes before presenting herself. Then she would refrain from mentioning anything about ice cream anymore. The thought of disappointing her mother was the last thing on her mind. Anything that could distract her would be the best remedy.

The Distraction

Chiddy hurried down the street, reluctantly, realizing she was in some inescapable trouble either way and tried to figure out what else to do. What would she tell Mother if she was awake and then found she took money?

Instantly, her interest charged with comfort when she saw some boys having a good time; it appeared cool, as if they were playing. They were having real fun, and she thought of reasons not to join them.

Quickly, she forgot everything. And for that short time, it felt great. But for how long? Would the problems have left?

As she approached them and told them her name, "Chiddy is my name," they rudely ignored her and kept doing whatever they were involved in before. Meanwhile, smiling away, she remembered that she intended to hide from the wrong thing done minutes ago but was somewhat distracted by whatever they were doing.

How wrong could she be? Watching what she thought were fun activities of the boys and preempting what they were doing from a distance, Chiddy was in for a rude surprise. Unfortunately, she

was mushroomed by their cold and feverish crude behavior toward another boy who was no stranger to them. He was a friend.

They were preoccupied with inflicting wounds on a small boy about her age, lying on the ground. He was crying his heart away, begging them to stop. His cry fell on deaf ears because they weren't even listening. He was trying to say something very important.

They halted the cruelty for a minute; she wondered why he screamed so loud as he could when he saw her. Seeing the boy crying on the ground was what bothered her the most. She asked them why he was crying. But no one cared to answer. And when she kept asking, one of the smaller, elfin boys interrupted by asking, "Who do you think you are? Why are you here?" Meanwhile, he gave her an angry, ugly, bulldog look.

And she was not afraid of them. Then she replied, "Why did you hurt him? What did he do?" She became confused. She wanted to find out why he was crying. The boys were laughing at the mean boy. "Ha, ha, ha!"

Another boy's crude, hard voice told her, "He is no longer our friend. He is terrible. He stole our friend's toy. We will teach him a lesson."

She gnashed at them, not believing what was said. *"Stop right there! What? Stole what? A toy?"*

"That's right."

"How sad."

But at the same time, she felt that the wrong thing she did went without saying and dunked her with regret. She also took what was not hers because she wanted ice cream badly. She couldn't wait and took it the wrong way.

She felt ashamed, knowing that it was only a toy the boy had taken.

"And it wasn't any different either because I also stole something and deserved punishment. It was only a dollar, but it felt like it was a million dollars."

Reluctantly, she did not want them to continue hurting him and tried to help. He got kicks and thumps while gazing at the bottom of their shoes in his face, head, and chest. And he refused to say another word. They called him mean and dirty names.

"Stop! stop!" the little girl demanded. "Hey! Leave him alone. Whatever you said he did—take an ugly, old toy?—that can be fixed easily. Stop and let us talk about it right now."

That's when they condemned him as a thief. "Zaka is a thief, and we must punish him for his actions."

Undoubtedly, the little girl remembered she was also a bigger thief who took her mother's one-dollar bill. What would the boys do with her if they found she was like a bank robber?

She asked, "How can you judge someone when we are all thieves? We are not without faults."

But they mocked and exclaimed, "We are not thieves."

"They said, "Yea, and we didn't do anything wrong!"

Surprisingly, they looked around at their friend, Antonio. He felt disappointed looking at the boys. Then he ran over and grabbed Zaka by the hand, lifted him, hugged him, and told him he was very sorry.

He looked at them and said, "What do you think? Yes, we did something wrong today."

Then Chiddy said, "You may have sinned and don't know. You might not steal but tell a lie. And more importantly, you might be very mean to others we are supposed to love."

They looked at each other sadly. They interrupted each other. "We have a lot of work, and they can understand it clearly."

Forgetful Friends

"He who is without fault, put your hands on him (cast the first stone)."

They realized how bad they were because he had no chance to explain. They didn't need to know if they were wrong.

Antonio forgot his toy on the playground the day before. He had yet to learn where he left it. However, Zaka saw the toy after Antonio left, knowing it was there by mistake; he took the toy to secure it for his friend.

But they misunderstood. Because as soon as they saw him with the toy, they forgot that they were best friends, and angrily, they rushed upon him to punish him. Why did they get angry when they saw him with the toy? Was it because they took it upon themselves to take out the wrongdoer?

Doesn't this sound familiar? The world is terrible because people want to punish others themselves. But the rules must be followed at all times. Is it important for someone to know the facts before making a hasty decision?

Chiddy's conscience was taunting her. She had to go home as quickly as possible to tell her mother what she had done. The little girl skipped hurriedly to tell Mom how sad she was.

"Mom! Come here. It is important, please come here! I must say something to you, Mom!" Chiddy looked at her mother and commented on how nice and tasty the ice cream could have been if she had done the right things already.

"Mother, I must be honest. I'm sorry for stealing the money from your purse to purchase this delicious ice cream. I wanted it badly. But after I got it and started eating, it wasn't so tasty or delicious anymore."

Mother was aware that Chiddy was missing, and watching from the back door, she figured she must have sneaked out to meet the truck. However, she wouldn't have said a word as yet. She was waiting to see if her daughter would prove herself an honest little girl as she taught her to be. If she had been dishonest, it would only break Mother's heart if she kept silent and said nothing about it.

She looked at her daughter and said, "It's okay because you are apologizing for something I had no idea about. The funny thing is I wouldn't miss one little dollar anyway. But you must appeal to God for forgiveness also. As long as you pray, the lesson will be learned when you ask for forgiveness. And I have a big surprise for you, dear. Wait until I tell you.

"You have been a wonderful daughter I love, and I wouldn't want to live without you. I want you to continue to work to the best of your ability, dear. We got the report from school yesterday, and I was not surprised to see the report cards. Well done, my child. How does a trip to see your sister sound to you?"

Chiddy passed her first test by speaking the truth and being honest about stealing Mom's money. She was excited when her mother announced that she would go to South Asia to spend time with her father and older sister.

The only drawback was the fear of the monsoons that played havoc in the southern countries of Asia. The thought of getting caught or trapped made her tremble.

However, Chiddy was determined that nothing would hamper her welcome trip. She knew she would enjoy all of it.

Look out for more kool, fun adventures as we will be taking a trip to the tropical exclusive scenery, views, and landscape of the southern islands of Asia.

39

About the Author

He loves nature and is keenly interested in various exotic birds. Thus, sightseeing is a motivating factor that captures his adventurous exploits. Poignantly, his trajectory to travel opens a grand horizon and catches his newfound friend, which offers an enthralling tapestry to expound his vocabulary in exchanging his thoughts in writing a new page.